SEP 1 2 2012

D1287394

WITHDRAWN

TEAM SPIRIT ®

SMART BOOKS FOR YOUNG FANS

THE CHICAGO BEARS

BY
MARK STEWART

NORWOOD HOUSE PRESS

CHICAGO, ILLINOIS

Norwood House Press
P.O. Box 316598
Chicago, Illinois 60631

For information regarding Norwood House Press, please visit our website at:
www.norwoodhousepress.com or call 866-565-2900.

All photos courtesy of Getty Images except the following:
Black Book Partners (4, 11, 14, 23, 24, 25, 35 bottom, 37, 39, 42 both, 43), Fran Byrne Photography (6),
Goudey Gum Co. (7), Topps, Inc. (9, 18, 30, 31, 35 top left, 36, 38, 45),
Chicago Bears/NFL (10, 20, 35 top right), Leaf Gum Co. (15), National Chicle (16, 34 left),
Little Brown (21), SCH Publications (22), Author's Collection (28, 33), Lance's Comic World (29)
TCMA Ltd. (34 right), Matt Richman (48).
Cover Photo: Icon SMI

The memorabilia and artifacts pictured in this book are presented for educational and informational purposes,
and come from the collection of the author.

Editor: Mike Kennedy
Designer: Ron Jaffe
Project Management: Black Book Partners, LLC.
Special thanks to Topps, Inc.

Library of Congress Cataloging-in-Publication Data

Stewart, Mark, 1960-
  The Chicago Bears / by Mark Stewart.
    p. cm. -- (Team spirit)
  Includes bibliographical references and index.
  Summary: "A revised Team Spirit Football edition featuring the Chicago
Bears that chronicles the history and accomplishments of the team. Includes
access to the Team Spirit website which provides additional information and
photos"--Provided by publisher.
  ISBN 978-1-59953-517-3 (library edition : alk. paper) -- ISBN
978-1-60357-459-4 (ebook) 1. Chicago Bears (Football team)--Juvenile
literature. I. Title.
  GV956.C5S74 2012
  796.332'640977311--dc23
                                          2012018317

Manufactured in the United States of America in North Mankato, Minnesota.
205N—082012

COVER PHOTO: The Bears celebrate a touchdown during the 2011 season.

Table of Contents

ABOUT OUR GLOSSARY

In this book, there may be several words that you are reading for the first time. Some are sports words, some are new vocabulary words, and some are familiar words that are used in an unusual way. All of these words are defined on page 46. Throughout the book, sports words appear in **bold type**. Regular vocabulary words appear in *bold italic type*.

Meet the Bears

As any wilderness expert will tell you, bears are powerful animals that can be extremely dangerous, especially when they feel threatened. The Chicago Bears can be described in a similar way. They take their name very seriously.

The Bears use speed and power to win, and the rougher the game, the more they seem to enjoy it. The Bears have been playing football this way for more than 90 years, and few teams have matched their record of success. No team in the **National Football League (NFL)** is more feared by its opponents, and no team is more loved by its fans.

This book tells the story of the Bears. It also tells the story of *professional* football. The NFL owes a lot to the Bears. They were the league's most admired team during tough times. Their owner and players changed the game. Much of what you see on the field today started with the great Chicago teams of the past.

Linebackers Brian Urlacher and Lance Briggs size up a Chicago opponent. The Bears are famous for their great defense.

Glory Days

In the early years of the 20th century, sports fans had little interest in pro football. They preferred the college game, where *amateurs* played for honor and glory. A businessman named George Halas believed that watching professionals play football was far more entertaining. In 1920, Halas convinced a group of business leaders to form a pro football league. It later became the NFL.

Halas played for and coached a team called the Staleys in Decatur, Illinois. Other stars for Decatur included Dutch Sternaman and Jimmy Conzelman. The Staleys eventually moved north to Chicago and changed their name to the Bears. Halas became the owner of the team at this time. He would later earn the nickname "Papa Bear."

In 1925, Halas and the Bears made a splash when they signed Red Grange, who was known across the nation as the "Galloping

Ghost." Grange thrilled fans with his long touchdown runs. After Grange's first season, Halas took the Bears on a coast-to-coast tour. Thousands and thousands of fans bought tickets to watch Grange play, and pro football began to gain national popularity.

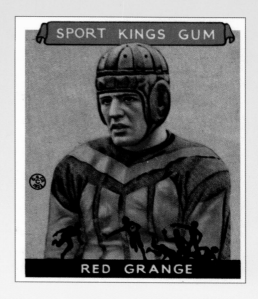

During the 1930s, Halas built his team into a powerhouse. The Bears won the NFL championship in 1932 and 1933. They also reached the title game in 1934 and 1937. Chicago's best player was Bronko Nagurski, an enormous runner who blasted through defenses. He was joined by three talented linemen—George Musso, Danny Fortmann, and Joe Stydahar—and an end named Bill Hewitt. Hewitt was one of the last NFL stars to play without a helmet.

The Bears were even better in the 1940s. Quarterback Sid Luckman led a high-scoring offense that included lineman Bulldog Turner, running back George McAfee, and receiver Ken Kavanaugh. The Bears played for the NFL championship every year from 1940 to 1943 and again in 1946. Chicago continued to win in the 1950s. The team's stars included Johnny Lujack, George Connor, Bill George, Harlon Hill, Stan Jones, Doug Atkins, Willie Galimore, and Rick Casares.

LEFT: George Halas diagrams a play for assistant Clark Shaughnessy during the 1950s.   **ABOVE**: Red Grange was Chicago's first superstar.

Many of these players were still on the team in 1963, when Chicago won its eighth championship. Later in the *decade*, two of the NFL's most remarkable stars played for the Bears. Dick Butkus was the most feared tackler in football. Gale Sayers had the best moves of any running back in the league. They were joined by Mike Ditka, the first tight end who was a great blocker and receiver.

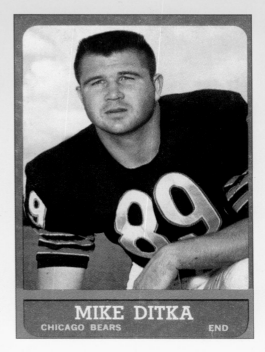

MIKE DITKA
CHICAGO BEARS   END

Despite this trio's contributions, the Bears struggled to remain a title *contender*. In the 1970s, stars such as Bobby Douglass, Richie Petitbon, and Wally Chambers gave fans lots to cheer about, but Chicago needed a new spark. In 1982, Halas hired Ditka to coach the Bears. Almost overnight, Chicago began playing winning football again.

Ditka built his offense around Walter Payton, a magnificent running back who combined speed and power in his own *unique* way. For many seasons, he was one of the few bright spots on the team. By the 1980s, Chicago had surrounded him with a lineup of talented players.

LEFT: Walter Payton makes a move to avoid a tackler.
ABOVE: Mike Ditka changed the position of tight end in the 1960s.

The Bears were ferocious on defense. They specialized in keeping other teams out of the end zone. Chicago relied on a group of **Pro Bowl** stars that included Dan Hampton, Steve McMichael, Gary Fencik, Dave Duerson, Richard Dent, and William Perry. The leader of the defense was Mike Singletary. The Bears went 15–1 in 1985 and won the **Super Bowl**.

During the 1990s, Chicago continued to play tough, physical football. Players such as Jim Harbaugh, Neal Anderson, Mark Carrier, and Chris Zorich gave championship efforts, but the Bears fell short of another title. In 2000, they found a new star in linebacker Brian Urlacher. He reminded many fans of Butkus. Urlacher played with great passion and knew how to fire up his teammates.

A few years later, the Bears hired Lovie Smith to be their coach. Smith was the first African American to lead the team. He focused on rebuilding the Chicago defense around Urlacher. Lance Briggs, Charles Tillman, and Tommie Harris all became stars under Smith. They helped form the heart of a defensive unit that carried the Bears back to the Super Bowl in 2007.

Three years later, the Bears were knocking on the championship door again. By then, Julius Peppers had joined the defense. Jay Cutler, Matt Forte, Devin Hester, and Greg Olsen led the offense. Each of these players brought something special to the field. Chicago advanced to the championship game of the **National Football Conference (NFC)** but lost to the Green Bay Packers. Bears fans were proud nonetheless. They knew that another championship was within reach.

LEFT: Mike Singletary
ABOVE: Brian Urlacher

11

Home Turf

For many years, the Bears shared Wrigley Field with the Cubs baseball club. In 1971, the team moved to Soldier Field in downtown Chicago. The stadium honors men and women who have fought in wars for the United States. It was **modernized** in 2002. After the stadium reopened, it ranked among America's best new buildings.

Chicago's stadium offers a great home-field advantage because it is located close to Lake Michigan. When the temperature drops in December and the wind whips off the water, the playing conditions get very chilly and uncomfortable for visiting players. On days like these, the weather is like a "12th player" for the Bears.

BY THE NUMBERS

- *The Bears' stadium has 61,500 seats.*
- *The stadium was first built in three stages from 1922 to 1939 at a cost of $13 million.*
- *The stadium's foundation includes 10,000 giant wooden stakes pounded deep into the ground.*

Four military aircraft fly over Soldier Field before a game.

Dressed for Success

George Halas is responsible for many of the team's *traditions*. That includes Chicago's famous navy blue and orange uniforms. He chose those colors because they were used by his college, the University of Illinois.

During the 1920s and 1930s, the Bears wore blue jerseys with orange stripes or orange jerseys with blue stripes. Often, the stripes were made of *canvas*, which helped players hug the ball securely against their bodies. In the 1940s, the team began using the deep blue color that it wears today. By the early 1950s, orange stripes had been added to the sleeves, pants, and socks. In 1970, player names appeared on the backs of the uniforms for the first time.

KEN KAVANAUGH

The Bears have used several different helmet colors over the years, including brown, black, blue, and white. In 1962, they added a large wishbone-shaped *C* *logo* to each side of their helmets. Chicago has featured different bears on its pennants and programs since the 1920s.

LEFT: Lance Briggs wears the team's road uniform.
ABOVE: Ken Kavanaugh catches a pass in the team's blue home jersey of the 1940s.

We Won!

The Bears have been a championship team since 1921. That year, they won their first title as the Staleys. Back then, there was no championship game. When the Bears finished with the best record in the league, they were crowned champions. The leader of the

BRONKO NAGURSKI

1921 team was George Halas. He was a player and the coach. Two of his stars were George Trafton and Guy Chamberlin. Trafton was the first center to snap the ball with one hand. He was also a great defensive player. Chamberlin was a talented receiver and runner who also excelled at defensive back.

Chicago's next championship came in 1932. By this time, defense ruled in the NFL—except in Chicago. The Bears were the league's highest-scoring team. Among their offensive stars were Bronko Nagurski, Red Grange, Bill Hewitt, Luke Johnsos, and Keith Molesworth. The Bears beat the Portsmouth Spartans 9–0 in a special **playoff game** for the championship.

The following year, the NFL was split into two **divisions**, East and West. The league scheduled a championship game between the division winners. The Bears took the West and faced the New York Giants in the NFL's first official title contest. Chicago won 23–21 on a great play in the fourth quarter. Hewitt caught a short pass from Nagurski, and then pitched the ball to Bill Karr, who ran the rest of the way for the winning touchdown.

The Bears won the West again in 1934 and 1937. Unfortunately, they lost in the championship games both times. In 1940, Halas assembled a new squad led by quarterback Sid Luckman, lightning-fast runner George McAfee, and Bulldog Turner, a great center and linebacker. Chicago met the Washington Redskins for the championship and wiped them out 73–0! The Bears rushed for 381 yards and seven touchdowns.

The Bears took the NFL championship again in 1941, 1943, and 1946. Luckman guided the way each season. Bill Osmanski

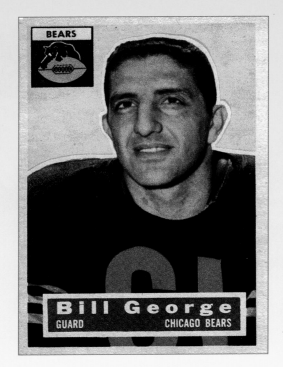

Bill George
GUARD   CHICAGO BEARS

was one of the top runners. The defense specialized in causing **turnovers**.

After Luckman retired, the Bears slowly rebuilt their team. In 1963, they won the NFL championship for the eighth time. That club was known for its great defense. Bill George, Ed O'Bradovich, Doug Atkins, and Richie Petitbon were strong tacklers who *pursued* the ball all over the field. The Bears gave up just 144 points during the regular season, and then defeated the Giants 14–10 in the title game.

Chicago fans had to wait more than 20 years for their next championship. In 1985, the Bears put together one of history's best seasons. Coach Mike Ditka's offense relied on the powerful blocking of Jim Covert and Jay Hilgenberg. They opened big holes for Walter Payton and gave quarterback Jim McMahon time to find open receivers. On defense, linebacker Mike Singletary was the leader of a unit that squeezed the life out of its enemies. Other defensive stars included Otis Wilson, Gary Fencik, Dave Duerson, Dan Hampton, Richard Dent, and a gigantic **rookie** named William "The Refrigerator" Perry.

The Bears finished the regular season at 15–1. In the **playoffs**, they shut out the Giants and the Los Angeles Rams. In Super Bowl XX, Chicago rolled over the New England Patriots. McMahon completed several long passes to Willie Gault, while Payton led a running attack that gained 167 yards. The Chicago defense punished the Patriots whenever they had the ball.

Chicago was up 37–3 in the third quarter when McMahon moved the team into scoring position. Near the goal line, he handed off to Perry, who was in the game for a special play. The "Fridge" slammed the door on New England with a one-yard touchdown run. The final score was 46–10.

LEFT: Bill George was the leader of the 1963 championship team.
ABOVE: The Bears carry Mike Ditka off the field after Super Bowl XX.

GO-TO GUYS

To be a true star in the NFL, you need more than fast feet and a big body. You have to be a "go-to guy"—someone the coach wants on the field at the end of a big game. Bears fans have had a lot to cheer about over the years, including these great stars …

THE PIONEERS

GEORGE TRAFTON   Lineman

- BORN: 12/6/1896   • DIED: 9/5/1971
- PLAYED FOR TEAM: 1920 TO 1932

George Trafton was one of the NFL's early "two-way" stars. He played center on offense and was one of the first defensive players to cover the field like a modern linebacker. Trafton was nicknamed the "Brute" because he was so mean and tough.

BRONKO NAGURSKI   Running Back/Linebacker

- BORN: 11/3/1908   • DIED: 1/7/1990   • PLAYED FOR TEAM: 1930 TO 1937 & 1943

Bronko Nagurski was the heart of the Bears during the 1930s. He could run, pass, block, and tackle as well as anyone in the NFL. Nagurski left football after eight seasons to become a professional wrestler. He later returned to the Bears and helped them win the 1943 championship.

DANNY FORTMANN   Lineman

- BORN: 4/11/1916   • DIED: 5/23/1995   • PLAYED FOR TEAM: 1936 TO 1943

Danny Fortmann was one of the greatest offensive linemen of his time. He was voted **All-Pro** every year he played in the NFL. After his career ended, Fortmann served as team doctor for the Los Angeles Rams from 1947 to 1963.

SID LUCKMAN   Quarterback

- BORN: 11/21/1916   • DIED: 7/5/1998
- PLAYED FOR TEAM: 1939 TO 1950

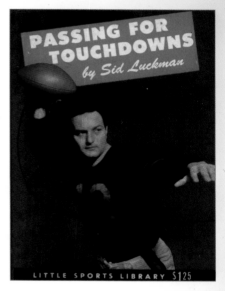

George Halas believed that passing was the future of pro football, and he needed a quarterback to master his system. Sid Luckman was his man. Luckman led the NFL in passing yards and touchdowns three times and guided the Bears to four championships during the 1940s.

BILL GEORGE   Linebacker

- BORN: 10/27/1929   • DIED: 9/30/1982   • PLAYED FOR TEAM: 1952 TO 1965

Bill George was the key to Chicago's ferocious defense in the 1950s and early 1960s. His ability to stop running backs in their tracks and cover pass receivers made him the NFL's first great middle linebacker.

MIKE DITKA   Tight End

- BORN: 10/18/1939   • PLAYED FOR TEAM: 1961 TO 1966

Mike Ditka was an excellent blocker and a gifted receiver. As a rookie, he caught 56 passes for 1,076 yards and 12 touchdowns. Later, he coached the Bears to the 1985 championship.

LEFT: George Trafton   **ABOVE**: Sid Luckman

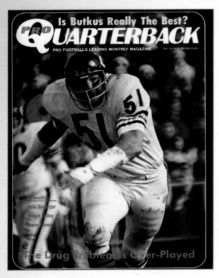

DICK BUTKUS   Linebacker

• BORN: 12/9/1942 • PLAYED FOR TEAM: 1965 TO 1973

Few players in NFL history could match the *intense* desire to win shown by Dick Butkus. Chicago fans loved him for his passion and fearless play. Butkus was voted into the **Hall of Fame** in 1979.

GALE SAYERS   Running Back

• BORN: 5/30/1943 • PLAYED FOR TEAM: 1965 TO 1971

Gale Sayers was known as the "Kansas Comet" because of his amazing speed. He could stop, change direction, and then restart before the defense had time to react. Sayers once scored six touchdowns in a game against the San Francisco 49ers.

WALTER PAYTON   Running Back

• BORN: 7/25/1954 • DIED: 11/1/1999 • PLAYED FOR TEAM: 1975 TO 1987

Walter Payton loved a hard-hitting football game—probably because he often hit tacklers harder than they hit him. Payton's quickness and strength helped him lead the NFC in rushing five years in a row. His friendly, soft-spoken nature earned him the nickname "Sweetness."

DAN HAMPTON   Defensive Lineman

• BORN: 9/19/1957 • PLAYED FOR TEAM: 1979 TO 1990

Dan Hampton stood 6′ 5″, weighed 265 pounds, and was nicknamed "Danimal" for his aggressive style of play. He often tied up two or three blockers, which allowed his teammates to take down the ball carrier.

MIKE SINGLETARY
Linebacker

- BORN: 10/9/1958
- PLAYED FOR TEAM: 1981 TO 1992

Mike Singletary was known as "Samurai Mike" because he played with frightening energy and intensity. He seemed to be everywhere at once and took it personally whenever an opponent scored. Singletary was voted All-Pro seven times from 1984 to 1991.

BRIAN URLACHER
Linebacker

- BORN: 5/25/1978
- FIRST YEAR WITH TEAM: 2000

Brian Urlacher followed the Chicago tradition of do-it-all linebackers. He was faster than most running backs, and offensive linemen couldn't block him one-on-one because of his quickness and power. Urlacher was the team's leading tackler almost every year he played and intercepted more than 20 passes in his career.

LANCE BRIGGS
Linebacker

- BORN: 11/12/1980
- FIRST YEAR WITH TEAM: 2003

Lance Briggs had great speed and *instincts*. He formed a perfect one-two punch with Brian Urlacher. When opponents focused their game plan on Urlacher, Briggs made them pay. He was picked to play in the Pro Bowl each year from 2005 to 2011.

LEFT: Dick Butkus
ABOVE: Brian Urlacher

23

Calling the Shots

George Halas was a *dynamic* leader who built the Bears into a championship team. He also was a driving force behind the NFL. In fact, many experts doubt whether the league would even exist had Halas not seen it through its early struggles.

Under Halas, the Bears were football's greatest team in the 1930s and 1940s. Halas was at his best when it came to designing plays on offense. He perfected the **T-formation**, which made quarterback the most important position on the field. He also saw the advantage of having full-time pass receivers in the lineup.

Halas coached the team for 40 seasons. At times, he stepped aside and let an assistant take over. The final season for Halas on

the sideline was 1967, but he continued to run the team as its owner. One of his best decisions was to hire Mike Ditka to coach the Bears in 1982. Halas believed the Bears needed a leader who shared his passion for the game.

Starting in 1984, Ditka led the Bears to the playoffs seven times in eight seasons. He became one of the most beloved sports figures in Chicago. Ditka built a powerful offense around running back Walter Payton and quarterback Jim McMahon. He turned the defense over to assistant coach Buddy Ryan. Ditka and Ryan did not always get along, but together they enjoyed great success.

Ditka guided the Bears to their first Super Bowl. The coach who led them to their second Super Bowl was Lovie Smith. He took over a losing team in 2004 and quickly whipped the Bears into shape, especially on defense. In 2005, Chicago allowed the fewest points in the NFL. In 2006, they became NFC champions.

One Great Day

As the Bears prepared to play the Washington Redskins for the 1940 NFL championship, fans expected a defensive battle. A few weeks earlier on Washington's field, the Redskins had beaten the Bears, 7–3. The game ended on a pass from Sid Luckman to Bill Osmanski that fell **incomplete** at the goal line. The Bears felt cheated. They argued that the Redskins had **interfered** with Osmanski.

Redskins owner George Preston Marshall boasted about his team afterward and told newspaper reporters that the Bears were "quitters" and "crybabies." This did not sit well with the Chicago players and coaches. They returned to Washington for the title game looking for revenge.

Coach George Halas and assistant Clark Shaughnessy had a trick up their sleeves. Their new T-formation would be a complete surprise to the Redskins. On the second play of the game, Osmanski sprinted 68 yards for a touchdown. The next time the Bears had the ball, Luckman led them into the end zone on a 17-play drive.

As the scoreboard shows, the Bears already had 60 points with just a few minutes gone in the fourth quarter.

Chicago scored twice more in the first half, on a 42-yard run by Joe Maniaci and a 30-yard pass from Luckman to Ken Kavanaugh.

The Chicago defense was terrific, too. In the third quarter, Hamp Pool, George McAfee, and Bulldog Turner each returned an interception for a touchdown. The Bears scored 28 points in the first half and added 45 more in the last two quarters to make the final score 73–0.

Halas and his players had smiles from ear to ear. Not only had they made Marshall eat his words, they had done so with millions of fans listening in. The 1940 NFL championship was the first pro football title game ever broadcast coast-to-coast on radio.

Legend Has It

Did the Bears make the NFL's first rap video?

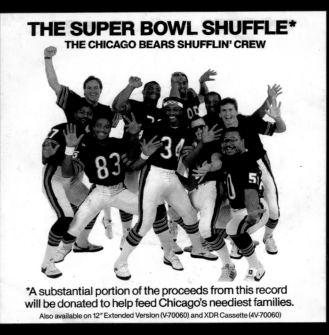

THE SUPER BOWL SHUFFLE*
THE CHICAGO BEARS SHUFFLIN' CREW

*A substantial portion of the proceeds from this record will be donated to help feed Chicago's neediest families.
Also available on 12" Extended Version (V-70060) and XDR Cassette (4V-70060)

LEGEND HAS IT that they did. During Chicago's amazing 1985 season, receiver Willie Gault convinced several teammates to record a rap song called "The Super Bowl Shuffle." They also made a video to go with it. Two of the team's stars, Walter Payton and Jim McMahon, were not available for the filming, so their parts were added in later. The song was a big hit, and much of the money it generated went to charity. A few months later, the song was nominated for a *Grammy Award*.

ABOVE: Willie Gault (#83) poses with his teammates for the cover of their rap record. RIGHT: Lance Briggs produced his own comic book in 2011.

Who was Chicago's quickest defensive player?

LEGEND HAS IT that Bill Hewitt was. Hewitt was one of the last NFL stars to play without a helmet. That did not keep him from becoming a great tackler. In fact, Hewitt had a special talent for darting between blockers and bringing down runners before they reached full speed. Opponents complained all the time that he crossed the **line of scrimmage** before the ball was hiked. Teammates thought this was funny. They called Hewitt the "Offside Kid."

Who was the NFL's biggest comic book fan?

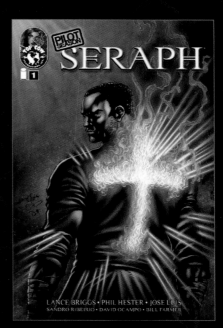

LEGEND HAS IT that Lance Briggs was. Briggs got hooked on comics as a boy and was a major X-Men fan. He continued buying comics twice a month as he got older. Briggs explained that reading a comic "was like creating a movie in my mind." In 2009, he launched his own comic book website, and two years later his first original title—*Seraph*—was published.

It Really Happened

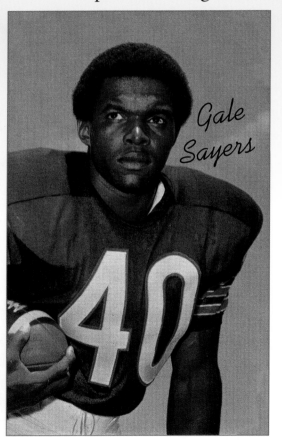

Gale Sayers

The Bears have been football pioneers since they first took the field in the 1920s. In 1967, the team made the most important change the NFL has ever seen. The Bears asked running backs Gale Sayers and Brian Piccolo to be roommates that year. Why was this such a big deal? Because Sayers was an African American and Piccolo was white. It was the first time that an NFL team had players of different races room together. The Bears knew this "experiment" would require two very special people.

Sayers was the NFL's most exciting runner. Piccolo had been a star in college, but no team drafted him because of his small size and lack of speed. The Bears decided to give him a chance to make their roster. Piccolo and Sayers ended up becoming best friends.

Bryon
PICCOLO
CHICAGO BEARS • RUNNING BACK

Sayers and Piccolo shared a hotel room during training camp and on road trips. Sayers challenged Piccolo to become a starting player, and he did. When Sayers suffered torn knee **ligaments** in 1968, Piccolo challenged him to become the first player to make a complete comeback from that type of injury. In 1969, Sayers returned to the Bears and led the NFL in rushing.

That season should have been one of triumph for the two friends. Instead, it turned out to be tragic. Piccolo had a bad cough that wouldn't go away. When he saw a doctor, he was told that he had lung cancer. Sayers stayed by Piccolo's side as he battled the disease. The two became even closer. Unfortunately, Piccolo died the following spring. In 1971, the film *Brian's Song* was made for television. It showed the uplifting friendship between the two players—and the heartbreaking loss suffered by Sayers and his teammates.

If you root for the Bears, you have to be tough. The weather in Chicago can be miserable, especially in the winter. However, Bears fans don't let it bother them. They show up for a game in the driving snow as if it were a perfect fall day.

Bears fans love to eat hearty meals before home games. They gather around Soilder Field for big tailgate parties that include all sorts of delicious foods. Sausage and Polish kielbasa are always favorites. So is the famous Chicago-style hotdog.

At Soldier Field, the fans are stirred to action by the Chicago Bears Drum Corps, the team's official drumline. They also cheer for Staley Da Bear. He is the perfect *mascot* for the club that so many fans fondly call "Da Bears." His first name also has a special meaning. When the team first came to Chicago, it was named the Staleys.

LEFT: Bears fans are loud, proud and very artistic.
ABOVE: This poster from the 1920s let fans know that special trains could take them to Bears games.

I n this timeline, each Super Bowl is listed under the year it was played. Remember that the Super Bowl is held early in the year and is actually part of the previous season. For example, Super Bowl XLVI was played on February 5, 2012, but it was the championship of the 2011 NFL season.

1932
The Bears win the NFL championship.

1946
The Bears win their fourth title of the decade.

1920
The Bears begin as the Decatur Staleys.

1934
Beattie Feathers is the first NFL player to rush for 1,000 yards.

1956
Rick Casares leads the NFL in rushing.

Beattie Feathers

Rick Casares

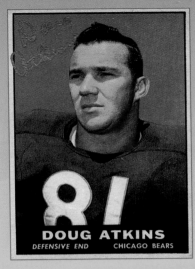

DOUG ATKINS
DEFENSIVE END   CHICAGO BEARS

Doug Atkins was
a star for the
1963 champs.

Jim McMahon
led the Bears to
Super Bowl XX.

1963
The Bears win their
eighth NFL championship.

1986
The Bears win
Super Bowl XX.

2011
Matt Forte is named
to the Pro Bowl.

1972
Quarterback Bobby
Douglass sets a record
with 968 rushing yards.

1980
Walter Payton leads the
NFC in rushing for the
fifth year in a row.

2000
Brian Urlacher is
voted Defensive
Rookie of the Year.

Brian
Urlacher

SOLD!

In 1922, the Bears needed to improve their blocking. George Halas purchased Ed Healey from the Rock Island Independents for $100. That made Healey the first NFL player acquired for cash.

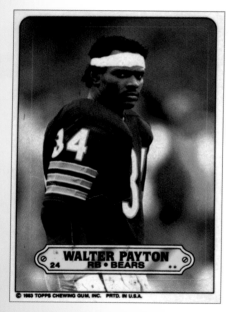

UNDER THE WEATHER

Walter Payton almost didn't play in a 1977 game against the Minnesota Vikings because he had the flu. It was the Vikings who ended up with a sick feeling that day. Payton ran for 275 yards to set a single-game record.

NO ORDINARY JOE

One of Chicago's best linemen in the 1930s was Joe Kopcha, who attended medical school during his playing days. He used his knowledge to redesign shoulder pads. Today every NFL player wears pads based on his ideas.

ABOVE: Walter Payton
RIGHT: Devin Hester

MANY HAPPY RETURNS

The Bears drafted Devin Hester in 2006 as a defensive back. They quickly found out that he was at his best with the ball in his hands. Hester returned three punts and two kickoffs for touchdowns as a rookie. In all, he had 18 returns for scores in his first six seasons.

ANOTHER FOOTBALL FIRST

The Bears had the NFL's first African-American quarterback, in 1953. He had the perfect name—Willie Thrower.

SHORT STORY

In 1932, the Bears and Portsmouth Spartans both finished the season at 6–1. A blizzard forced the tie-breaking game indoors at tiny Chicago Stadium. The playing field actually had to be shortened to 60 yards. The Bears won 9–0 and took the NFL championship.

ULTIMATE ALL-STAR

Gale Sayers was probably the best player in the history of the Pro Bowl. He was the game's offensive MVP three times. In 1967, Sayers ran for 110 yards on only 11 carries. He also had runs of 55 yards and 80 yards that were wiped out because of penalties.

Dick Butkus

"The trick was to figure out what someone was going to do before they did it. I learned to read those details as part of my survival."

► **Dick Butkus,** *on how he made so many tackles*

"Nobody who ever gave his best regretted it."

► **George Halas,** *on playing with effort and pride*

"If I get my best shot, I don't see how a guy can hold onto the ball."

► **Mike Singletary,** *on his talent for causing fumbles*

"I never saw anyone hit the line so hard."

► **Sid Luckman,** *on Bronko Nagurski's running style*

"We had a strange and wonderful relationship. He's strange and I'm wonderful!"

▶ **Mike Ditka**, *on Jim McMahon*

"I don't care to be remembered as the man who scored six touchdowns in a game. I want to be remembered as a winner in life."

▶ **Gale Sayers**, *on being a great person as well as a great player*

"I'm a competitor. I want to win. That's why you go out there and play."

▶ **Jay Cutler**, *on what motivates him on the field*

"They've had some great ones here—Butkus, Singletary, and Bill George—but I'm not trying to be like them. I'm just trying to be me."

▶ **Brian Urlacher**, *on how he compares to other Chicago linebackers*

LEFT: Dick Butkus
ABOVE: Mike Ditka discusses a play on the sideline.

Great Debates

People who root for the Bears love to compare their favorite moments, teams, and players. Some debates have been going on for years! How would you settle these classic football arguments?

Walter Payton was Chicago's greatest player ...

... because he was the NFL's all-time rushing champion. But more than that, he was an amazing all-around star. Fans forget that he could also catch passes and throw them. Payton (LEFT) held the record for career receptions by a running back and also passed for eight touchdowns. He was a great team player, too. When Payton wasn't handling the football, he could usually be found blocking for someone who was.

Mike Singletary wins this battle ...

... because the Bears have always been about defense, and Singletary was their greatest defensive star. In the 1980s, Chicago had the NFL's top defense. It was built around Singletary at middle linebacker. No one was better at stopping running backs, and few linebackers were better at covering receivers. Singletary was Defensive Player of the Year twice, in 1985 and 1988.

The 1942 Bears were Chicago's greatest team ....

... because they had a perfect 11–0 record. After beating the Green Bay Packers on opening day, the Bears didn't allow more than two touchdowns in any game the rest of the season. Four of their 11 wins came by shutout. Sid Luckman, Bulldog Turner, Danny Fortmann, George Wilson, and Lee Artoe were at the peak of their powers. Not a single one of the team's games was even close that year!

Forgetting something? The 1985 Bears were NFL champions ....

... because their defense was *dominant*. Chicago won 15 games during the regular season in 1985, and then rolled over their opponents in the playoffs. In Super Bowl XX, the Bears destroyed the New England Patriots. William Perry (RIGHT) was a perfect example of how talented the Bears were. Against the Patriots, he helped Chicago's defense hold New England to just seven rushing yards, and he scored a touchdown on a run of his own. Plus, don't forget that the 1942 Bears didn't win the championship. They lost the title game to the Washington Redskins.

For the Record

The great Bears teams and players have left their marks on the record books. These are the "best of the best" ...

Mark Carrier

Anthony Thomas

BEARS AWARD WINNERS

WINNER	AWARD	YEAR
Sid Luckman	Player of the Year	1943
Doug Atkins	Pro Bowl co-MVP	1959
Mike Ditka	Offensive Rookie of the Year	1961
Ronnie Bull	Offensive Rookie of the Year	1962
George Halas	Coach of the Year	1963
George Halas	Coach of the Year	1965
Gale Sayers	Offensive Rookie of the Year	1965
Gale Sayers	Pro Bowl co-MVP	1967
Gale Sayers	Pro Bowl co-MVP	1968
Gale Sayers	Pro Bowl co-MVP	1970
Wally Chambers	Defensive Rookie of the Year	1973
Walter Payton	Most Valuable Player	1977
Walter Payton	Offensive Player of the Year	1977
Walter Payton	Pro Bowl MVP	1978
Mike Singletary	Defensive Player of the Year	1985
Mike Ditka	Coach of the Year	1985
Richard Dent	Super Bowl XX MVP	1986
Mike Singletary	Defensive Player of the Year	1988
Mark Carrier	Defensive Rookie of the Year	1990
Brian Urlacher	Defensive Rookie of the Year	2000
Dick Jauron	Coach of the Year	2001
Anthony Thomas	Offensive Rookie of the Year	2001
Lovie Smith	Coach of the Year	2005
Brian Urlacher	Defensive Player of the Year	2005

BEARS ACHIEVEMENTS

ACHIEVEMENT	YEAR
NFL Champions	1921*
NFL Champions	1932
NFL Western Division Champions	1933
NFL Champions	1933
NFL Western Division Champions	1934
NFL Western Division Champions	1937
NFL Western Division Champions	1940
NFL Champions	1940
NFL Western Division Champions	1941
NFL Champions	1941
NFL Western Division Champions	1942
NFL Western Division Champions	1943
NFL Champions	1943
NFL Western Division Champions	1946
NFL Champions	1946
NFL Western Conference Champions	1956
NFL Western Conference Champions	1963
NFL Champions	1963
NFC Central Champions	1984
NFC Central Champions	1985
NFC Champions	1985
Super Bowl XX Champions	1985**
NFC Central Champions	1987
NFC Central Champions	1988
NFC Central Champions	1990
NFC Central Champions	2001
NFC North Champions	2005
NFC North Champions	2006
NFC Champions	2006
NFC North Champions	2010

* Team played as the Chicago Staleys
** Super Bowls are played early the following year, but the game
is counted as the championship of this season.

ABOVE: Dan Hampton went to the Pro Bowl for the fourth time following the 1985 season.

43

Pinpoints

The history of a football team is made up of many smaller stories. These stories take place all over the map—not just in the city a team calls "home." Match the pushpins on these maps to the **Team Facts**, and you will begin to see the story of the Bears unfold!

TEAM FACTS

1. Chicago, Illinois—*The Bears have played here since 1921.*
2. Pittsfield, Massachusetts—*Brian Piccolo was born here.*
3. Connellsville, Pennsylvania—*Johnny Lujack was born here.*
4. Jersey City, New Jersey—*Jim McMahon was born here.*
5. Riviera Beach, Florida—*Devin Hester was born here.*
6. Wilson, North Carolina—*Julius Peppers was born here.*
7. New Orleans, Louisiana—*The Bears won Super Bowl XX here.*
8. Gladewater, Texas—*Lovie Smith was born here.*
9. Oklahoma City, Oklahoma—*Dan Hampton was born here.*
10. Wichita, Kansas—*Gale Sayers was born here.*
11. Pasco, Washington—*Brian Urlacher was born here.*
12. Rainy River, Ontario, Canada—*Bronko Nagurski was born here.*

Devin Hester

Glossary

🧠 **ALL-PRO**—An honor given to the best players at their positions at the end of each season.

🧠 **AMATEURS**—People who play a sport without being paid.

🧠 **CANVAS**—A type of strong, heavy fabric.

🧠 **CONTENDER**—A team or person who competes for a championship.

🧠 **DECADE**—A period of 10 years; also specific periods, such as the 1950s.

🧠 **DIVISIONS**—Groups of teams that play in the same part of the country.

🧠 **DOMINANT**—Ruling or controlling.

🧠 **DYNAMIC**—Exciting and energetic.

🧠 **GRAMMY AWARD**—An honor given to people in the music industry.

🧠 **HALL OF FAME**—The museum in Canton, Ohio, where football's greatest players are honored.

🧠 **INCOMPLETE**—Hit the ground before being caught.

🧠 **INSTINCTS**—Natural ways of acting or thinking.

🧠 **INTENSE**—Extremely strong or serious.

🧠 **INTERFERED**—Illegally prevented a receiver from catching a pass.

🧠 **LIGAMENTS**—Bands of tissue that connect bones.

🧠 **LINE OF SCRIMMAGE**—The imaginary line that separates the offense and defense before each play begins.

🧠 **LOGO**—A symbol or design that represents a company or team.

🧠 **MASCOT**—An animal or person believed to bring a group good luck.

🧠 **MODERNIZED**—Brought up to date.

🧠 **NATIONAL FOOTBALL CONFERENCE (NFC)**—One of two groups of teams that make up the NFL.

🧠 **NATIONAL FOOTBALL LEAGUE (NFL)**—The league that started in 1920 and is still operating today.

🧠 **PLAYOFF GAME**—A game played after the regular season that determines a league champion.

🧠 **PLAYOFFS**—The games played after the regular season to determine which teams play in the Super Bowl.

🧠 **PRO BOWL**—The NFL's all-star game, played after the regular season.

🧠 **PROFESSIONAL**—Paid to play.

🧠 **PURSUED**—Chased.

🧠 **ROOKIE**—A player in his first year.

🧠 **SUPER BOWL**—The championship of the NFL, played between the winners of the National Football Conference and American Football Conference.

🧠 **T-FORMATION**—An offensive set in which three running backs line up in a row behind the quarterback to form a "T."

🧠 **TRADITIONS**—Beliefs or customs that are handed down from generation to generation.

🧠 **TURNOVERS**—Fumbles or interceptions that give possession of the ball to the opposing team.

🧠 **UNIQUE**—Special or one of a kind.

OVERTIME

TEAM SPIRIT introduces a great way to stay up to date with your team! Visit our **OVERTIME** link and get connected to the latest and greatest updates. **OVERTIME** serves as a young reader's ticket to an exclusive web page—with more stories, fun facts, team records, and photos of the Bears. Content is updated during and after each season. The **OVERTIME** feature also enables readers to send comments and letters to the author! Log onto:

www.norwoodhousepress.com/library.aspx

and click on the tab: **TEAM SPIRIT** to access **OVERTIME**.

Read all the books in the series to learn more about professional sports. For a complete listing of the baseball, basketball, football, and hockey teams in the **TEAM SPIRIT** series, visit our website at:

www.norwoodhousepress.com/library.aspx

On the Road

CHICAGO BEARS
1410 South Museum Campus Drive
Chicago, Illinois 60605
847-295-6600
www.chicagobears.com

THE PRO FOOTBALL HALL OF FAME
2121 George Halas Drive NW
Canton, Ohio 44708
330-456-8207
www.profootballhof.com

On the Bookshelf

To learn more about the sport of football, look for these books at your library or bookstore:

- Frederick, Shane. *The Best of Everything Football Book.* North Mankato, Minnesota: Capstone Press, 2011.

- Jacobs, Greg. *The Everything Kids' Football Book: The All-Time Greats, Legendary Teams, Today's Superstars—And Tips on Playing Like a Pro.* Avon, Massachusetts: Adams Media Corporation, 2010.

- Editors of *Sports Illustrated for Kids. 1st and 10: Top 10 Lists of Everything in Football.* New York, New York: Sports Illustrated Books, 2011.

Index

PAGE NUMBERS IN **BOLD** REFER TO ILLUSTRATIONS.

About the Author

MARK STEWART has written more than 50 books on football and over 150 sports books for kids. He grew up in New York City during the 1960s rooting for the Giants and Jets, and was lucky enough to meet players from both teams. Mark comes from a family of writers. His grandfather was Sunday Editor of *The New York Times,* and his mother was Articles Editor of *Ladies' Home Journal* and *McCall's.* Mark has profiled hundreds of athletes over the past 25 years. He has also written several books about his native New York and New Jersey, his home today. Mark is a graduate of Duke University, with a degree in history. He lives and works in a home overlooking Sandy Hook, New Jersey. You can contact Mark through the Norwood House Press website.